THE SECOND COMPLETE IRISH GAG BOOK

A Star Original

Anglo-Irish Garry Chambers (English on his mother's side and Irish on a friend of his father's) is one of Britain's most prolific comedy writers. His T.V. credits include 'The Bob Hope Show', 'Bruce's Big Night', 'Faith Brown Chat Show' and 'Who Do You Do?'

*Almost

Also by Garry Chambers in Star

THE *COMPLETE IRISH GAG BOOK

*Almost

THE SECOND *COMPLETE IRISH GAG BOOK

Compiled by Garry Chambers

Illustrated by Bill Tidy

*Almost

A STAR BOOK

published by
the Paperback Division of
W. H. ALLEN & Co. Ltd.

A Star Book
Published in 1980
by the Paperback Division of
W. H. Allen & Co. Ltd
A Howard and Wyndham Company
44 Hill Street, London W1X 8LB

Printed in Great Britain by
Hunt Barnard Printing Ltd., Aylesbury, Bucks.

ISBN 0 352 30640 8

My thanks to Carla Zanetti for her
help in preparing the manuscript.

THE SECOND *COMPLETE IRISH GAG BOOK

*Almost

THE IRISH AT HOME

PREPARING FOR A NIGHT OUT

'For heaven's sake, Maureen, how much longer are you going to be?'

'Sean, I've been telling you for over an hour that I'll be ready in a minute.'

DINNER

'How are the fish fingers, Sean?'

'Maureen, they melt in my mouth.'

'Damn, I knew I should've cooked 'em after I took 'em out of the freezer.'

Voice on Irish telephone answering machine: Speak when you hear the green light.

'Just clean the inside of the windows, Maureen, not the outside, so's we can look out at the neighbours but they can't look in.'

Murphy always wears his cap in the bathroom so he'll know where to stop when he washes his face.

Did you hear about the Irishman who bought his godson a christening shovel?

Maureen: Sean, wipe that filthy muck off your boots.
Sean: What boots?

'Hey Maureen, I thought we were going to have spaghetti for dinner.'

'So did I, Sean, but my saucepan isn't long enough.'

Sean and Tim were watching an edition of *This Is Your Life*. Remarked Sean, 'You know, Tim, men like Eamonn Andrews are a dying breed who will live forever.'

Hearing a crash from the kitchen, Maureen called out, 'Sean, have you broken my new salad bowl?'

Yelled back Sean, 'Only in parts, Maureen, only in parts!'

Irish navvy: Kate, why are my work socks full of holes?
Wife: Well, you asked me to boil them and I had to keep prodding them with a fork to see if they were done.

Murphy came home from work early and found his missus in bed with three of his mates. 'Hello, hello, hello!' he exclaimed.

Retorted his wife, 'What's the matter, Murphy, aren't you speaking to me?'

'What do you want for breakfast, Sean?'

'Oh, Maureen, boil me two three-minute eggs.'

'I don't have time to boil two, so you'll just have to make do with one.'

Murphy had his ear amputated so his landlord couldn't throw him out on it for non-payment of rent.

There's a village in Ireland so small that the barbershop quartet has only three members.

THE MORNING AFTER

'Oh, stop moaning, Maureen. I was especially quiet when I came home last night.'

'Yes, *you* were, but the two fellers who carried you upstairs weren't.'

Regan was on his deathbed. He and his missus had raised five kids; four were really beautiful, and one was as ugly as sin. This had disturbed Regan since the child was born. Hoping to clear up the matter before he passed away, he asked his wife, 'Tell me, Peggy, our fifth child, is he really mine?'

'Oh yes, he's yours all right,' admitted Peggy. 'Mind you, the other four aren't.'

Did you hear about the Irish housewife who thought you could tell the age of an onion by counting the rings?

'Sean, I wish we could afford a new TV set. The programmes we get on this old one are terrible.'

Deidre wants to be a straight actress and she has a pretty good chance because her vital statistics are 32-32-32.

'Sean, the goldfish is dead.'

'Funny. It was okay last night when I put it back in its cage.'

Littlewoods rep: Good morning, sir, have you done the pools?
Irishman: No, it's my dog.

Tramp: Can you give me a slice of bread?
Irish housewife: Do you mind yesterday's?
Tramp: No.
Irish housewife: Then come back tomorrow.

Ninety per cent of Irishmen wear wellies. The other ten per cent have learned how to tie boot laces.

FRONT DOOR VISITOR

'Mrs Riley, tell your husband that Murphy is here to beat him to a pulp!'

'Oh, I'm terribly sorry, Murphy, my husband's not at home.'

Murphy noticed a nail sticking out of his front door. So he removed the door and carried it up to the attic because that was where he kept the pliers.

'Hey, Maureen, why are you cutting that block of ice into little cubes?'

'So they'll fit into the ice tray.'

Irish party game: Pin The Horns on the Donkey.

'Well, Maureen, I'd like to stand here gossiping with you a bit longer but I don't have the time.'

'It's a quarter to twelve.'

'You know, Maureen, I won't believe in colour television till I see it in black and white.'

Housewife: Come in, but please be careful as I've just waxed my brand new vinyl floor.
Irish meter reader: Oh, I won't slip over, missus, I'm wearing spiked shoes.

Little Tommy tucked into a Sunday lunch of roast chicken and stuffing. 'Mum,' he suddenly asked, 'why is it chickens only eat sage and onion?'

Maureen: Sean, will you buy me one of those Continental bidets?
Sean: A Continental bidet? Is that one of those things for washing a baby in?
Maureen: No, it's for washing a baby *out*!

'What's that you're erecting in your garden, Sean?'

'It's a bird bath.'

'A bird bath? You mean those little creatures actually know when it's Saturday night?'

Then there was the Irishman who sneezed so violently that his nostrils fell out.

Maureen and her fancy man were making love in the bedroom when they heard someone coming in the front door.

'My God,' gasped the lover, 'is that your husband?'

'Oh, don't let it bother you,' shrugged Maureen. 'He can't fight either!'

'You know, Sean, the goldfish must be very happy today.'

'What makes you say that?'

'Well, just look at it. It's wagging its tail.'

Then there was the Irish bachelor who washed the wrong side of his hanky.

'You know, Kelly, that Murphy is getting to be a real snob. He's got ashtrays in his house with no advertising on them.'

'I won't be long in getting changed for the dance, Sean. Wait for me as quickly as you can.'

Fireman: Tell me, Murphy, how did your bed catch fire?
Murphy: Search me. It was already on fire when I got into it.

Then there was the depressed Irishman who decided to kill himself with an overdose of aspirin. However, after taking the first two he felt much better.

Did you hear about the Irishman who went looking for a gas leak with a safety match?

'Hey, Maureen, this meringue tastes funny.'

'Well, I made it according to the recipe. It said to separate two eggs, so I left one egg on the kitchen table and the other one on the window ledge.'

'Hurry up and finish breakfast, Sean, I want to lay the table and serve lunch.'

Maureen: Is the baby still crying, Sean?
Sean: It's okay, Maureen, he's just started to stop.

Then there's the Irish egg-timer that's an hour fast.

'Hey, Maureen, who switched the TV set back off?'

Household hint: In hot weather, put a bucket of manure in the centre of the dining table to keep the flies off the food.

Did you hear about the Irishman who had a bowl of wax fruit?
It went rotten.

'Hey, Mum, I've just made some mud pies.'
'Well, Tommy, make sure you wash your hands before you eat them.'

TV Licence Detector Official: May I see your TV licence, please?
Irish householder: Can you come back tomorrow after I've bought one?

'Hey, Sean, what are you using as bait in your mousetrap?'
'The cat.'

Did you hear about the smallest village in Ireland?
It's so tiny that they take it indoors when it rains.

Sean met Tim in the street. Tim was carrying a crate of Guinness. 'Going to a party?' asked Sean.
'No,' replied his friend. 'Moving house.'

DINNER TIME

'Well, Sean, how's the bread and butter pudding?'

'Oh, the bread and butter's fine, Maureen, but I don't think much of the pudding.'

And what about the Irish housewife who bought a pound of soya mince and asked for the bone for her dog?

Salesman: Good morning, madam, is your husband in?
Maureen: Just a minute, I'll ask him.

If you have a gas leak in your home, put a bucket under it and send for the Gas Board.

Did you hear about the Irishman who came home drunk one night so his wife beat his head in with the Welcome mat?

'Maureen, don't give the baby a new dummy till she's finished eating the one she has now.'

Then there was the Irishman who stared at a veal, ham and egg pie and wondered how they got the chicken to lay the egg right in the centre.

Murphy was on his deathbed. 'Maureen,' he gasped, 'before I go, can I have a piece of that chocolate cake you baked this afternoon?'

'You certainly cannot,' retorted his wife. 'I'm saving that for the wake!'

Then there was the unhappy gypsy boy who plans to run away from home just as soon as his mum and dad get one.

THE IRISH AT WORK

Irish maternity hospitals have a twelve-month waiting list.

Then there was the Irish gardener who tried to kill moles by burying them alive under the lawn.

When Maureen was a lot younger she worked as a cover girl. For manholes.

CAR SHOWROOM

'Does this car have a guarantee?'
'Oh yes, sir, we guarantee it's a car.'

In Dublin a one-man bus crashed while the driver was up-stairs collecting fares.

Foreman: Murphy, you'll have to do that wall all over again.
Murphy: And why's that?
Foreman: You've put the paint on upside down.

Then there was the Irish dredging crew who went out to the site of the sunk *Titanic* and raised the iceberg.

Did you hear about the Irish level crossing attendant who kept one gate open because he was half expecting a train?

Then there was the Irish boxer who was so crooked, he took a dive shadow boxing.

Dublin window cleaners have a collection and delivery service.

Irish builder: I'm sorry, missus, but I can't lay you a concrete path today. I've left my ladders back at the yard.

Then there was the Irish traffic warden who ticketed 125 cars till he realised he was at the Motor Show.

PET SHOP

'That dog you sold me has distemper.'

'Well, what do you expect for a mongrel? Crown Gloss?'

In Irish postal sorting offices the word 'Fragile' means 'break it gently'.

At Dublin's General Hospital a house doctor sat down to write out a prescription and discovered he was holding a rectal thermometer. 'Damn!' he exclaimed. 'Some bum's got my Biro.'

Then there was the Irishman who was so short he got a job as a hod carrier for Leggo.

'Are you a pawnbroker?'
'Yes.'
'Well, where's your sign?'
'I pawned it.'

Two Irish navvies were working on a demolition site near Heathrow Airport. Shouted Pat, 'My nerves can't take much more of this noise!'
'Don't worry,' yelled back his friend, 'Concorde will fly over in a minute and drown it out!'

DUBLIN UNDERTAKER'S

'I want you to bury my wife.'
'Yes, sir. Just a minute, I'm sure I buried your wife six months ago.'
'That's right but I remarried.'
'Oh, congratulations.'

Personnel officer: Okay, you've got the job as chef. We'll pay you £90 a week plus your food.
Irishman: What, no luncheon vouchers?

BLACKSMITH'S

Irish blacksmith: All right, you've got the job as my assistant. Can you start right away?
Youth: Okay, but what do I have to do?
Irish blacksmith: You hand me the horses.

Did you hear about the Irish tube train driver who was sacked for overtaking?

Personnel officer: Any experience of book keeping?
Irish applicant: Oh yes, sir, I've got three novels overdue from the library.

BUILDING SITE

'You're late, Murphy.'
'Sorry, Boss, but I fell down stairs.'
'In that case you should've been early!'

This Irish navvy had been constipated for a month so he went to his doctor. The doctor examined the patient's backside and suggested he get it unblocked by asking a navvy mate to have a go at it with a pneumatic drill. Puzzled, the navvy asked what good that would do. The doc told him it would break up some concrete which was attached to his back passage.

'Oh, and another thing,' added the doctor, 'from now on, every time you go to the toilet on the building site, don't wipe yourself on a discarded cement bag.'

'Hey, Sean, are you still working as a dog catcher?'
'Oh no, Tim, I packed that job in after a week. I knew I had to catch dogs but nobody told me what I had to catch them *at*!'

The Irish Post Office have solved the vandalism problem by making all the telephone boxes Ex-directory.

Dublin sex shop manager: I've imported a lot of bondage equipment but it's all tied up at the docks.

Then there was the Irish navvy who accidentally got locked in the building site privvy and didn't find out about it for two whole hours.

PHONE CALL TO A DEPARTMENT STORE

'How late does your restaurant stay open?'

'Sorry, sir, you have the wrong extension. This is the Information Desk.'

Murphy got a job with British Rail. So, first day at work, he turned up in a track suit.

Did you hear about the Irish church bellringer?
Every time the bell rang he yelled out, 'Come in!'

Then there was the Irish navvy whose steamroller got a puncture.

Murphy the glassblower inhaled suddenly and got a pane in the stomach.

DUBLIN FLORIST'S SHOP

'How much are your bunches of flowers?'
'You mean a 50p bunch or a £1 bunch?'
'A 50p bunch.'
'50p, but I don't have any left. I can split a £1 bunch for you.'
'Okay.'
'Fine. Do you want the petals or the stems?'

Irish tailor to customer: What's your inside waist measurement?

STATIONERY SHOP

'I want a twelve-inch ruler.'
'Small, medium or large?'

There's a café in Dublin where the food is so bad they have a sign on the door which reads 'Sorry, We're Open.'

Then there was the Irish gypsy who had a highly lucrative job selling horse manure. So lucrative in fact, that when he died he left quite a pile.

Irish tree surgeon to tree: Cough!

Notice on wall of office corridor: Toilet out of order. Please use floor below.

Then there was the Irish chicken farmer who went broke because a heavy frost killed all the eggs he'd planted.

Then there was the Irish schoolboy who got O levels in Maths and Art. When he left school he got a job painting cash registers.

Boss: You can't expect a rise after being with the firm only a week. You've got to work yourself up.
Murphy: But I am, Boss. I'm trembling all over.

Murphy applied for a job as a park litter collector. He admitted he had no experience but said he would pick it up as he went along.

DUBLIN FLORIST'S

'Those flowers you sold me yesterday were dead.'
'I know. I thought you wanted them to make a wreath.'

Murphy got a job in the ticket office of Leeds station. His first customer was a man who simply said, 'Return – King's Cross.'

Retorted Murphy, 'Return King's Cross? How the hell can I if I never took it in the first place?'

Murphy rushed into a hardware shop and shouted, 'Give me a mousetrap, quick, I've got to catch a bus!'
'Sorry,' retorted the sales assistant, 'but our traps won't catch anything bigger than a rat.'

Did you hear about the Irish astronomer who got fired because he wouldn't work nights?

Irish gravediggers have gone on strike but will still handle emergencies.

'Hey, Sean, I've just been offered a job as a precision engineer. Only trouble is, I've got to be able to measure things in thousandths of an inch.'
'My God. How many thousandths are there in an inch?'
'I don't know but there must be millions.'

Foreman: Okay, Murphy, you got the job. Now how much do you want a week?
Murphy: Two hundred pounds.
Foreman: Two hundred pounds? But you're unskilled.
Murphy: Yes, but the job is always much harder when you don't know anything about it.

Sign in Dublin factory canteen: All drinking water in this establishment has been passed by the company's health officer.

Irish gravediggers threatened to go on strike and caused a wave of panic dying.

Then there was the Irish fortune teller who was reading a palm when she fell out of the tree.

Personnel officer: What's your typing speed?
Irish secretary: Thirty words in small letters and fifteen in capitals.

Customer: Give me the five-minute friction treatment.
Irish barber: Right, sir. Won't take me half a second.

Personnel officer: Right, you've got the job as Chief Accountant. It pays a salary of £5,200 a year.
Irish applicant: How much is that a week?

Irish traffic wardens have yellow lines round their caps to stop motorists parking on their heads.

DUBLIN OFF LICENCE

'Bottle of Irish whiskey, please.'
'Sorry, it's being held up by the Dublin dock strike.'

DUBLIN TAILOR'S SHOP

'I want you to make me a suit but I don't want any pockets, lapels, buttons, buttonholes, lining or vents.'
'Ah, that'll be twice my normal price.'
'Why twice?'
'Well, it's for all those extras.'

In a Dublin court a barrister was fined for perjury because he referred to the opposing council as 'my learned friend'.

A Dublin supermarket manager resigned and joined the priesthood where he eventually got his own church. The first thing he did was install an Express Confessional for parishioners with eight sins or less.

LADIESWEAR SHOP

'Can I boil this wool sweater?'
'Yes, but only boil it in *warm* water.'

DUBLIN CHEMIST SHOP

'Can you make me something up?'
'Raquel Welch came in here this morning for a pair of falsies.'
'Really?'
'No, I just made it up!'

Irish driving instructor to pupil: Today I'll teach you how to reverse forwards.

Then there was the Irish tree surgeon who committed adultery with one of his patients and had to marry it.

LABOUR EXCHANGE IN WINTER

'I can offer you a job driving a snow plough.'
'What, in this weather?'

Then there was the Irish plastic surgeon who specialised in repairing Tupperware.

Then there was the Irish fan dancer who got electrocuted because the fan wasn't properly earthed.

Did you hear about the Irish postman who looked everywhere for a round letter box so he could deliver a circular letter?

Small ad: Nightwatchman wanted. Seven days off a week.

PHONE CALL TO THE BOSS' OFFICE

Female voice: Is my husband there?
Irish secretary: No. Who shall I say phoned?

Then there was the Irish postman who resigned because he said the new postal codes were too difficult to pronounce.

Irish fishmonger: My fish are so fresh, you'll have to drown 'em before you can cook 'em.

Then there was the Irish second hand car dealer who turned back all the fuel gauges.

THE IRISH OUT AND ABOUT

CHEMIST'S SHOP

'Packet of Pyrex, please.'
'Don't you mean Durex?'
'No, I've got a date with a hot dish.'

Murphy lost his Post Office Savings Bank book in Dublin. Three days later it was found by the Police but £100 had been deposited in it.

DUBLIN BANK

Molly: Can you give me two fifty pence pieces for this English pound note?
Clerk: This isn't an English pound note, it's a soap coupon.
Molly: My, God, I've been raped!

An Irishman burst into a dentist's surgery brandishing a gun. Waving the weapon at the dentist he snarled, 'Pull all my teeth out! No gas, no needle, no nothing! And pull 'em, out slowly.'

'But,' reasoned the dentist, 'there's nothing wrong with your teeth. And anyway, if I pulled them out slowly one by one without any anaesthetic, the pain would be unbearable.'

Jabbing the gun in the man's ribs, the gunman yelled, 'Do as I say or you're dead!'

Trembling, the dentist pulled the Irishman's teeth out, slowly and without anaesthetic. When the final extraction had been completed, the Irishman jumped out of the dentist's chair and pulled the trigger. From out of the gun barrel came a flag with the word 'BANG' written on it. As he ran from the dentist's surgery, he shouted, 'April Fool, I only wanted a haircut!'

Travelling home late one night Sean was waved down by a policeman just outside Dublin who told him his right head-light was off. Thanking the officer, Sean restarted his motor-bike and continued on his way.

Did you hear about the Irish rugger player who was offered a trial with the British Lions. He turned up for training at Longleat.

DUBLIN FLORIST'S SHOP

'What's that?'
'A rubber plant.'
'Really? Whereabouts do you pump it up?'

There's a town in Ireland so small that after they hired a traffic warden they had to hire some traffic.

Murphy, on his way home late on Saturday night, reached for a cigarette and someone trod on his hand.

'Excuse me, but where's the nearest pub?'
'Oh, seven miles away. Unless you go in the other direction, in which case it's only two hundred yards.'

The *early* part of Murphy's marriage was okay. The trouble started as he and his bride were leaving the church.

Irish tourist: I've written my name and address on both sides of my luggage label in case it comes off.

Then there was the Irish motorist who, on seeing his first set of snow tyres said, 'How the hell do they get all that snow through the inner tube valve?'

Murphy, famous for his stinginess, saw a blind man begging with a tin cup. Dropping a ten pence coin in the cup he told the man it was a fifty pence piece and took forty pence change.

U.S.A.

Policeman: Hey, buddy, don't you know it's against the law to have a gun in this state?
Irish hunter: What do you mean? I had it overhauled only last week.

Murphy went to the zoo and had to buy two tickets. One to get in and one to get out.

Did you hear about the Irish soccer team who scored a goal and declared?

Murphy staggered out of his local at closing time and threw up all over a passing dog. Looking down at the wretched animal he said, 'Funny, I don't remember eating that!'

Then there was the Irish pickpocket who was caught in the act. The cops used the snooker table as evidence.

Then there was the Irishman on a motoring tour of Scotland who pulled into a garage and asked for a set of Mull of Kin tyres.

DUBLIN DANCE HALL

Dancer: Play *In the Mood.*
Bandleader: We just played it.
Dancer: I wish I'd known. It's my favourite tune.

'Well, Murphy, how's your insomnia?'
'Improving, doc. Most days I have better nights than not.'

Magistrate: Thirty days or ten pounds.
Criminal: I'll take the ten pounds.
Magistrate: I'd like time to pay.

DUBLIN CHINESE RESTAURANT

'Do you do takeaways?'
'Yes. Six take away three leaves three.'

MIRROR SHOP

'Does this mirror reflect in black and white or colour?'

Irishman: Doc, I'd like some glasses for work.
Optician: Okay, what's your job?
Irishman: I'm a heavyweight boxer.

ELECTRICITY SHOWROOM

'I bought a cooker from you last week and it's useless. The little light inside the oven takes ages to bake a cake.'

Then there was the Irishman who was so lazy he once fell asleep during a Saturday night punchup.

Policeman: Blow into this bag!
Drunk driver: Which end?

Mrs Murphy is so fat that she went to Weight Watchers on a scholarship.

DUBLIN HOTEL

Tourist: I'm from England and I'm used to having the best of everything.
Receptionist: Well, the change here will do you good.

Murphy went into a branch of Irvine Sellers and asked the salesman to sell him an Irvine.

Then there was the Irishman who walked into a restaurant, sat down at a table, called the waiter over and said, 'I'm in a hell of a hurry. Just bring me the bill!'

What's an Irish disco?
A ward full of St Vitus Dance sufferers.

CONFESSIONAL

'Forgive me, Father, for I have sinned. I just smashed a shop window and punched three policemen.'

'But why?'

'Well, I knew I was coming here but didn't have enough sins to confess.'

PHONE CALL TO THE IRISH COASTGUARD

'Hello? I was out in the bay when my boat sank.'

'Capsize?'

'Six and seven-eighths.'

A Dublin cop stopped a motorist who was driving the wrong way down a one-way street. 'Hey,' exclaimed the policeman, 'don't you know this is a one-way street?'

'Well,' reasoned the driver, 'I'm only going one way, aren't I?'

At a recent Irish wedding, the bride was so ugly that everyone kissed the groom.

In Irish schools the three 'R's are Geography, Latin and History.

Then there was the Irish show jumper who broke his nose jumping against the clock.

First Irish hunter: If I miss the bird with my first shot I always hit it with my second.
Second Irish hunter: Well, to save cartridges, why not fire the second shot first?

Did you hear about the Irish skydiver who was disqualified for missing the ground?

HOSPITAL

'How did you become a doctor?'
'Oh, I started as a patient and worked my way up.'

'You know, Sean, after we lost last Saturday's soccer game by ten goals to nil, the Captain took me to one side and told me I was the team's drawback.'
'Drawback? What position is that?'

Then there was the young Irish couple who had a society wedding. The catering was done by the Co-op.

DUBLIN STATIONERY SHOP

'A packet of envelopes, please.'
'Manilla ones?'
'Hell, no! Give me some that were made here in Ireland.'

Two Irish homos: William Fitzpatrick and Patrick Fitz-william.

DUBLIN GENERAL HOSPITAL

'Well, Kelly, I'm afraid you've got sugar in your water.'

'But I'm a diabetic. What's so unusual about my having sugar in my water?'

'Cubes?'

CAR DEALER'S SHOWROOM

'Do you do part exchange?'

'Yes.'

'Well, I'd like to exchange my new car for an old part.'

The Irish pound is so worthless that anybody spending one is asked to write his name and address on the back of it.

Then there was the Irishman who broke his leg in an Ear, Nose and Throat Hospital.

Ireland's top TV Western: Have Gun, Will Lose It.

Then there was the Irish celebrity who died of shock when Eamonn Andrews said to him, 'This Is Your Life!'

'Where'd you go for your holidays, Sean?'
'Palermo.'
'Where's that?'
'I don't know. I flew there.'

Then there was the Irish politician on *Mastermind* who answered all Magnus's questions with the phrase 'No comment'.

Murphy saw a large sign over a restaurant which read 'Mrs Gilhooley's Home Cooking'. He went in and asked when she'd be back.

'Sean, it says on this firework "Light blue touch paper".'
'So?'
'Well, the touch paper is *dark* blue.'

Mrs Murphy saw a notice in the supermarket window which read, 'Buy two toilet rolls and get one free.' She went inside and asked which was the free one.

POLICE STATION

'Officer, I've been mugged. The mugger stole my wallet.'
'I see, sir, and what time did this happen?'
'I don't know. He stole my watch too.'

Sign in amusement arcade: Madam Zaza – Fortune Teller. Minds read £5. Irish minds read for half price.

MENSWEAR SHOP

'A pair of trousers, please.'
'Yes, sir, that'll be £10.'
'Oh! I've only got a fiver. Let me have half a pair instead.'

Murphy went into a pub and asked the barman for a drink with a little body in it. The barman served him a glass of wine containing a dead fly.

Last Christmas Murphy and his missus went window shopping and came home with six windows.

NEWSAGENT

'A *Radio Times* and a *TV Times*, please.'
'Sorry, *TV Times* is on strike.'
'Well, give me two copies of *Radio Times*, then.'

Irish wedding photographer: I'm sorry but I can't take a photo until you all get into focus.

Then there's the Irish cat. Whichever way you throw it, it always lands on its head.

Warning for shipping: Off the West Coast of Ireland is a five-mile wide gas-slick.

Murphy heard that MacDonald's was a fast food restaurant so he went in and gobbled down a Big Mac in three and a half seconds flat.

CHEMIST SHOP

'Do you have a shampoo that stops falling Brylcreem?'

Then there was the Irishman who was so mixed up he had a twinkle under his arm and a shillelagh in his eye.

Did you hear about the Irishman who was arrested for making hoax calls to the Speaking Clock?

Murphy: Can you take me home to 85 Galway Street?
Dublin cabbie: Hell no, it's so foggy I'd never find it.
Murphy: Don't worry. I'll walk ahead of you and you can follow me till we get there.

LONDON

Irish tourist to wife: Now remember, Molly, if we lose each other, you stay right where you are and so will I.

'Sean, what's the most you can get out of your car?'
'Well, so far this morning I've had to get out of it fifteen times.'

Then there were the two queer Irish ghosts who gave each other the willies.

IRISH CONCORDE

Pilot's voice: Ladies and gentlemen, we have just flown from London to Dublin in three minutes.
Passenger: Is that a record?
Pilot's voice: No, this is the pilot speaking.

Then there was the Irishman who walked all the way from John O'Groats to Land's End to join the start of the long distance walking race.

Did you hear about the two Irish queers who registered at a hotel as Mr & Mr Smith?

'I hear that Muldoon went to Mexico for a holiday and was killed by a black widow spider. Did it bite him?'
'Well, it didn't kick him to death.'

'Hey. Sean, are those two dogs Jack Russells?'
'No, one's mine and the other one's my brother's.'

Dublin's Post Office Tower has a revolving restaurant where the customers run round in circles and the waiters throw food at them.

How can you spot an Irish teddy boy?
His sideboards are *behind* his ears.

Then there was the Irishman who donated a pint of blood to the local blood bank. That's a half pint from each eye.

Newspaper headline: Fifty Irish Clairvoyants Killed In Coach Crash.

RED LIGHT AREA

'Like a nice time?'
'How much?'
'Twenty pounds.'
'American Express?'
'You can do it as fast as you like.'

Did you hear about the Irish motorist who, every ten thousand miles, changed the air in his tyres?

Then there's the Irish cat that does its business and then buries itself.

Sean's sister was emigrating so he went to evening classes to learn how to wave goodbye.

HOSPITAL

'Mr Kelly, I've got to change the dressing on your leg.'
'Okay, nurse. Do you have any Thousand Islands?'

Did you hear about the Irish sheepdog?
It didn't have fleas, it had moths.

A recent survey reveals that between 50,000 and 80,000 Irish females have excess body hair. These are, of course, rough figures.

DUBLIN PUB

'Your glass is empty, sir. Want another?'
'Now, just why would I be wanting *two* empty glasses?'

MATERNITY HOSPITAL WAITING ROOM

'I'm a father, I'm a father! Have a cigar.'
'Thanks. Is it a boy or girl?'
'I don't know. All cigars look alike to me.'

Then there was the Irishman who returned a half-used bag of cat litter to the pet shop complaining that no matter how he served up the stuff, his cat just wouldn't eat it.

Policeman: Didn't you see that sign that said 'Maximum Speed 25 Miles An Hour'?
Irish motorist: Hell no, Officer, I was driving much too fast to read it.

Did you hear about the Irishman who went to Mothercare to be measured up for a paternity suit?

Irish con man: I own Blarney Castle, but I'll sell it to you for a million pounds.
U.S. tourist: Nuthin' doin'.
Irish con man: Okay, then I'll give you fifty quid to take it away.

How can you spot fashion-conscious Irish girls?
They wear split-sided tights and stiletto-heeled wellies.

HOSPITAL WARD

'What are you in for?'
'Appendectomy.'
'Your first?'

Irish danceband leader: And now, me and the lads will play a slow quickstep.

Did you hear about the Irishman who thought Max Head Room was the owner of a chain of underground car parks?

'Is it foggy out?'
'Foggy? It's so foggy that you can't see your hand behind your back.'

'Hey, Sean, can you speak Dutch?'
'Only enough to chat up a sick elm tree.'

Miss Ireland's vital statistics are 36-22-36. And the other leg's the same.

THE RIVER LIFFEY

Drowning Irishman: I can't swim! I can't swim!
Passing Irishman: So what? I can't play the piano but I don't shout about it!

Personnel officer: We're looking for someone who's honest, reliable and not afraid of hard work.
Irish applicant: Well, you employ me, sir, and I'll help you look.

Then there was the Irishman who was so dull, Polaroid photos of him took two hours to develop.

Irish hippy to customs officer: How much marijuana am I allowed duty free?

DEPARTMENT STORE

'Do you sell monogrammed hankies?'
'Yes we do. What initial would you like?'
'What do you suggest?'

Then there was the Irish bank robber who pulled a stocking over his head . . . and a lady's shoe.

Then there were the two Irishmen who played snooker. After half an hour they still hadn't potted the red so they took the triangle off.

TV commentator during snooker game: For those of you watching in black and white, the red ball is next to the green one.

DUBLIN THEATRE

Latecomer: Any empty seats?
Commissionaire: Yes, sir, but they're all full.

Then there was the Irish girl who was so thin that her boobs were in single file.

Seaside landlady: You can have a room overlooking the bay for £25.
Irish tourist: How much is the room if I promise not to look?

POLICE STATION

'My juggernaut's been stolen, has one been handed in?'

'No, sir, but we'll round up some suspects and search them.'

Sign in Dublin chemist's shop: Ears pierced. Special offer. Pay for two and get another ear pierced free.

Then there was the Irish golfer who hit a ball in one.

Did you hear about the Irishman who didn't realise he had diarrhoea until he took off his cycle clips?

And you'll be delighted to know that the Irish Boat People have just sailed into Vietnam.

Did you hear about the Irish actor whose ambition was to play the title role in *Waiting For Godot*?

Then there was the short-sighted Irishman who dropped his cigar outside Battersea Dogs Home. He picked up and lit fifteen of them till he discovered the right one.

Opening line of Irish mind reader to audience: Any requests?

Irish flood warning sign: When the water level rises above this sign please phone Dublin 3850097.

Did you hear about the overweight Irishwoman who was told by her doctor to watch her waistline so she went out and tried to buy a see-through girdle?

Did you hear about the Irishman who lost a contact lens when the putty fell out of his eye?

MURDER SCENE

'Any clues found near the body, Sergeant?'
'Yes, Inspector, a gun.'
'Where is it?'
'We're holding it for questioning.'

Did you hear about the Irish gambler who was banned from all Dublin casinos because he had a foolproof losing system?

New magistrate: Murphy, I hear you get drunk quite often.
Murphy: Sorry, your honour, sir, I'll get drunk much quieter from now on.

DUBLIN RESTAURANT

'I can recommend the wood pigeon, sir.'
'Really? What flavour is the wood?'

Irish sport: Water skiing through a car wash.

'Paddy Murphy, I arrest you for breaking into Number Ten Downing Street.'
'Jeez, officer, how did you catch me so quickly?'
'You shouldn't've signed the Visitors' Book.'

Murphy and Kelly went on holiday to Paris and sat down at a pavement café for a meal. Feeling faint, Kelly asked his pal to help him out into the fresh air.

There's no prostitution in Ireland because, let's be honest, you only have to look at Irish girls to realise they can't even *give* it away.

A Las Vegas casino has a very plush domino room. So luxurious is the equipment that the spots on each domino are real diamonds. When no one was looking, an Irish gambler stole a double blank.

Irish seaside rock has the words 'Open other end' all the way through it.

The Irish Mafia caught a spy and cut his tongue out to make him talk.

Then there's the one about the Irish aircraft carrier. He ruptured himself lifting the plane out of the hangar.

DUBLIN OPTICIAN'S

'Well, Sean, how are you managing with your new contact lenses?'

'Terrible, doc. I can't get 'em on over my glasses.'

Then there was the three-fingered Irish thief who could only steal bowling balls.

How do you spot an Irishman in a bowling alley?
He's the one bowling *overarm.*

Things move so slowly in Ireland that the population uses the same calendar two years running.

DUBLIN UNIVERSITY

Angry lecturer: Riley, are you listening to me?
Daydreaming student: No, sir! Cross my heart!

Irishman to girlfriend: Your dad's just given me two black eyes. I'm going home before he gives me two more!

Murphy bought a pair of spiked plimsolls because his doctor told him he had the runs.

Useful address: The Secretary, Irish Samaritans, 12th Floor Window Ledge, St Patrick House, Dublin.

Ireland's National Sports: Soap Box Grand National, Stock Plane Racing, Scrambled Egg and Spoon Racing.

'Hey, Sean, I've taken up tennis.'
'Really? What position do you play?'

Then there was the Irish vandal who went to the cinema, hated the film, pulled out a knife and slashed his bum.

Magistrate: Murphy, why did you steal a hammer, a pair of wellies and a transistor radio?
Murphy: Well, your honour, I was hungry.

Then there was the Irish boy scout who had to stop doing good turns because they made him dizzy.

Dublin publicans call last orders on dog whistles.

Then there was the Irish mugger who wore white wellies so he wouldn't leave footprints in the snow.

Then there was the Irish jellyfish that set.

Which reminds me of the Irish aquarium enthusiast who bought a Portuguese man-of-war but it surrendered.

Did you hear about the Irishman who tried to grow a handlebar moustache but it kept falling off the front of his bike?

Sign in Dublin health food shop: Try our herbal remedies. You can't get better.

SWINGING SINGLES BAR

Girl: Hey, I like you. Why not come back to my place and we'll have a great time. I've got a bedroom with mirrors on the walls and mirrors on the ceiling. Oh, by the way, you'd better bring a bottle.
Irishman: But where the hell am I going to get Windolene at this time of night?

Irish old lag to judge: Your Honour, since my last stretch I've bent over backwards trying to go straight.

The Irish Round The World Yacht Race has just been announced. If wet, it'll be held indoors.

Then there was the Irish sprinter who was lapped in the 100 yards race.

SURGERY

'How's your bladder, Murphy?'
'Okay, doc, as bladders run.'

Good news. Irish Skylab has landed and the hijacker has surrendered.

CHEMIST'S SHOP

'A packet of moth balls, please.'
'Anything else?'
'Yes, do you sell catapults?'

'Sean, do you drink Guinness?'
'Well, what else can you do with it?'

Do you know how to spot an Irishman in a cinema showing a foreign film?
He's the one using his finger to read the subtitles.

THE WIT AND WISDOM OF THE IRISH

Irishman with four leaf clover: She loves me, she loves me not, she loves me, she loves me *not*. Damn! Who says these things are lucky?

'Oh, Maureen, how sad that Mick and Bianca Jagger got a divorce. And after all those years of not being together.'

Irish Roulette is rather like Russian Roulette but instead of a gun you beat yourself over the head with a shillelagh six times. Once very hard.

'O'Riley's dead. Are you going to his funeral?'
'I'd better, otherwise he won't go to mine.'

Did you hear about the Irishman who thought Sandeman Port was where the ships dock in the Sahara Desert?

'Do you like my new brown shoes, Tim?'
'I certainly do, Sean. I've got a black pair the same colour at home.'

Did you hear the one about the Irish cat?
It died and left all its money to an old ladies home.

'You know, Sean, the price of petrol is now so high I just can't afford it.'

'Well, why don't you do what I do? No matter how much it costs it still doesn't affect me.'

'How's that?'

'Simple, I buy it by the pound's worth.'

Did you hear about the Irishman who thought an autobiography was the life story of a motor car?

Irish Goldilocks: Who's been sleeping in my porridge?

'You know, Sean, those silicon chip watches are ahead of their time.'

'They are? Now why the hell would anyone want to buy a watch that's fast?'

'My doctor's put me on those birth pills Molly, but they're useless. They keep dropping out.'

Then there was the Dubliner who thought blackmail was a West Indian postman.

What did the Irish queer say to the Irish Guardsman?
Hello, sailor.

Murphy thinks a cubic foot is what develops if you eat too many Oxos.

Murphy thought a Palestinian guerilla was an ape from the Holy land.

Rodney: By the way, old chap, did you hear the joke about the Irishman who . . .
Sean: Just a minute, boyo, *I'm* Irish!
Rodney: Really? Well, in that case I'll tell it to you very slowly. Twice.

Then there was the Irishman who thought the Master of the Rolls was a loo attendant.

Did you know that Dublin is the largest city of its size in Ireland?

'Hey, Maureen, there's a hole in this sock.'
'Well, wear it inside out and no one will notice.'

Did you hear about the Irishman who thought a logarithm was a birth control record for Catholics.

The letters T-U-F on Tuf boots stand for Toes Up Front.

A new Irish digital watch on the market shows the date, the hour, the minute, the second and how much time is left before the pubs shut.

TV series about an Irish private eye: *Wellystring*.

Small ad. in Irish pop music paper: For Sale, Elvis Presley's death certificate personally autographed by the King himself. Genuine. £5 each or two for £9.

'Sean, would you say you were indecisive?'
'I'm not sure.'

Then there was the Irishman who thought Sherlock Holmes was a housing estate.

'Sean, have you seen the Dead Sea?'
'Dead? I didn't even know it was sick. When is the funeral? Or is it being cremated?'

'You know, Maureen, you're getting awfully thin lately.'
'Yes, I know. I've put on a loss of weight.'

Then there was the Irish woman who gave birth to a test tube baby and asked the Doctor if she should breastfeed the kid washing-up liquid.

'Constable, I've just seen a UFO.'

'Really, Mrs Murphy? And how can you be sure it was a UFO?'

'Because it had the letters UFO painted on each wing.'

Did you hear about the Irish flagpole sitter who broke the world record by staying up there for three years and fifty days? Unfortunately, he died on the final day so they lowered him down the flagpole to half mast.

SCHOOL

'Please, Miss, where do the words go to when you rub them off the blackboard?'

Then there was the Irish navvy on an oil rig who, every morning, would check to see if the helicopters had laid any eggs.

Why has a glass of Guinness a white head on it?
So the Irish will know which end to drink first.

'Is your grandfather still alive, Sean?'

'No, Tim, he's still dead.'

Cop: Murphy, you're drunk!
Murphy: You wouldn't dare say that to me if I was sober!

Newspaper headline: Oxford and Cambridge Reach Final of Boat Race.

'Hey, Sean, come quick! Paddy's drowning in the Liffey. Fetch him a glass of water!'
'But, Tim, what's he want a glass of water for if he's drowning?'
'Well, every little helps!'

Then there was the Irishman who committed suicide by slipping arsenic in his tea while looking the other way.

'What's your star sign, Sean?'
'Oh, us Areans don't believe in astrology.'

Did you hear about the Irishman who, during the 1976 drought, helped out by only drinking dry martinis?

Then there was the Irishman who thought Bob Marley and the Wailers were the sailors who caught Moby Dick.

'You know, Molly, my life is such a mess that if it wasn't for my valium, librium and nembutal, I'd be on drugs.'

'How's your husband, Sally?'
'He died.'
'Oh, I am sorry.'
'That's all right. It was nothing serious.'

The Irish National Anthem: Sing Something Simple.

Then there was the Irishman who thought Sheffield Wednesday was a bank holiday.

SWEET SHOP

'I don't like those mints with the holes in them.'
'Then just eat the mints and spit the holes out.'

Then there was the Irishman who thought a taxidermist was someone who stuffs cab drivers.

Murphy wants to know where people who live in Lourdes go when they're sick.

Then there was the Irishman who thought Boogie Fever was a nasal complaint.

ROAD ACCIDENT

Ambulance driver: Can you tell me your name so I can let your wife know.
Irish victim: But my wife already *knows* my name.

'You know your trouble, Sean, you've got a persecution complex.'
'You're just saying that because you hate me.'

Then there was the Irishman who was so clumsy he could even spill Vaseline.

Irish radio programme: Phone-in for the Deaf.

Then there was the Irishman who was so unlucky, he bought a walking stick which developed a limp.

PHONE CONVERSATION

'Hello, is that you, Tim?'
'Yes, who's that?'
'Sean.'
'Listen, Sean, I can't talk now, I'm in the middle of a phone call.'

Then there was the Irishman who thought that 'The great smell of Brut' was the Incredible Hulk's B.O.

The Irish are great believers in health. They're forever drinking to other people's.

Small ad. Paperweight for sale. Good working order.

'Hey, Tim, have you and your wife a family yet?'

'Alas no. Ten years married and no children. We've tried everything too.'

'Oh yes? How's your sex life?'

'Sex? Hey, what a great idea!'

Then there was the Irishman who thought camiknickers were thieves who stole toilet soap.

Sean: Who's your village idiot, Tim?
Tim: Oh, we take it in turns.

According to Ireland's Health Department, thanks to modern medicine, more people are dying healthier than ever these days.

Irish perfume: O'De Colleen.

Irishman's motto: When the cat's away, kick something else.

Irish captain of Titanic*:* Iceberg overboard!

Small ad.: Bedsitter for rent. Kitchen but no bathroom. Would suit Irish navvy.

'Hey, Sean, can you stand on your head?'
'Jeez no, Tim, it's too high up.'

'Do you think they should bring back hanging for murder?
'Only if the murder results in death.'

Did you hear about the Irishman who thought the Cote d'Azur was a blue jacket?

Then there was the Irish yachtsman who had his arm off so he could sail round the world single-handed.

Not to be confused with the Irish musician who had *both* arms off so he could play the piano by ear.

'You know, Sean, I think Pat is a twin.'
'What makes you say that?'
'Well, I heard him say he has a photo taken when he was two.'

'What are you wearing to the dance tonight, Maureen?'
'Oh, Rosie, I usually wait till I'm dressed and then decide.'

Did you hear about the Irishman who went into a fabric shop and asked for a refill for his felt tip pen?

Irish doctor: Mrs Murphy, I'm afraid your husband is at death's door. But don't worry. You can rely on me to pull him through.

DUBLIN RESTAURANT

Waiter: Anything else, sir?
Diner: Yes, bring me a very small bill.

SEASIDE HOLIDAY

'Sean, if you fall off that cliff you'll be dead for the rest of your life.'

'What's the idea of bringing my daughter home at five in the morning?'
'Well, Mr Kelly, I have to be at the building site by six.'

Then there was the Irishwoman who was so nosey she was afraid to blink in case she missed something.

'You know, Sean, that Murphy, he's a real villain.'
'That he is. I bet his parents are glad they never had any children.'

Irish limbo dancer: You'll have to lower the pole. I can't jump over it when it's that high.

'Hey, Sean, where've you been?'
'The cemetery.'
'Oh, really? Who's dead?'
'They all are!'

I won't say Murphy is thick but he paid £150 for the Unknown Soldier's autograph.

Did you hear about the Irish secret agent who wrote all his messages in invisible Braille?

Irish birth control song: Hit Me With Your Rhythm Mick.

Which reminds me of the slogan for Irish contraceptives: Better sorry than safe.

Murphy is so lazy he applied for a job as a used sugar salesman.

'Maureen, how many men have you kissed before me?'
'Oh . . . er . . . er . . . '
'I'm still waiting.'
'I'm still counting.'

'Hey, Sean, who did you vote for in the last election?'
'Oh, I never vote, Tim, it only encourages them.'

Sartorial tip for well-dressed Irishmen: Always keep cuff-links in your shirt cuffs to prevent the holes healing up.

Written on bottles of Irish Optrex is the warning: Keep away from eyes.

Then there was the Irishman who thought Father Christmas was a Catholic priest.

Then there was the Irish carpenter who went into an iron-mongery store and asked if they sold Rockford files.

Sean to antique dealer: Hello, Mike, what's new?

'Tim, why are you making faces at the goldfish?'
'Well, he started it.'

Did you hear about the Irish conservationist who went into business making imitation donkey jackets?

Then there was the Irishman who thought Royal Enfield was the Queen's chicken run.

'Sean, who are your two favourite TV personalities?'
'Ask and Jimal.'
'Who the hell are Ask and Jimal?'
'Those two fellers, Ask Aspel and Jimal Fixit.'

What do you call a good-looking Irishman?
Lucky.

'You know something, Sean, platinum is very valuable. In fact, it's worth it's weight in gold.'

Did you hear about the Irishman who developed a double chin?
He grew a double beard to hide it.

Irish film: *Escape to Alcatraz.*

Irish description of condoms: Wellies for willies.

'Hey, Sean, are you queer?'
'Listen, just because I go to bed with queers, doesn't mean I am one!'

Then there was the Irish gambler who lost £5000 playing Patience.

'Oh, Mrs Francis, my Maureen is getting married.'
'Married, Mrs Ryan? I didn't even know she was pregnant!'

'Did you sleep well last night, Sean?'
'Oh, I slept *twice* as well!'
'*Twice* as well?'
'Yes, I dreamed I was asleep!'

'Tell me, Sean, are the Clancy Brothers really brothers?'
'Oh yes. And so are the Nolan Sisters.'

Then there was the Irishman who had worms. Rather than waste them, he went fishing.

Article in Irish medical journal: 'Are Vasectomies Hereditary?'

If it hadn't been for the invention of the bowling ball, you'd have to run down the bowling lane and kick the pins down with your feet.

Irish author: I may be unknown outside Ireland but back home in Ballymena I'm world famous.

Maureen to her naughty triplets: You three are a right pair if ever I saw one.

'Molly, I don't like your new boyfriend's appearance.'
'Oh, that's not fair Mum. You can't tell someone's appearance just by looking at them.'

'You know, Sean, the BBC's Open University is a brilliant scheme. I've learned things I never knew.'

'Pardon me but where's the cemetery?'
'Dead ahead.'

Did you hear about the Irishman who thought Midnight Express was a credit card you could only use after dark?

Then there was the Irishman who woke up in hospital in a terrible state. 'Doctor, doctor,' he wailed, 'I can't feel my legs. Please don't tell me you've amputated them!'
'For heaven's sake stop worrying,' replied the doctor. 'It's your arms we had to take off.'

'Murphy's such a liar, when he says "Good morning" I switch the light off and go to bed.'

Sign in Dublin department store: Kid gloves for sale. Suit any size kid.

Did you hear about the manic depressive Irish coward who committed suicide by shooting himself in the back?

Maureen: I won't say my Tommy's hopeless when it comes to his school exams, but he has to cheat to come last.

During the lavatory paper shortage of a few years ago, a Dublin chemist put a notice in his window which read: 'Toilet rolls for regular customers only.'

'Good news, Murphy, we've found your stolen car and all your stuff in the boot is still there.'

'Oh, that's just great, constable. Thank God the thief was an honest man.'

'Hey, Maureen, how are you feeling these days?'

'Terrible, Rosie, terrible. One of these nights I'll wake up in the morning and find myself lying there dead.'

PHONE CALL

Callee: Dublin 32796011.
Caller: Idiot! You've got the wrong number!

Did you hear about the Irish gangster on his deathbed who confessed to ten murders and then recovered?

'Sean, I've been looking at our financial state and we owe over four hundred pounds.'
'Don't worry, Maureen, we'll borrow enough money to get us out of debt.'

Then there was the Irish down-and-out who was addicted to drinking Harpic and went clean round the bend.

'Oh, Sean, the doctor's given me a year to live.'
'Don't worry, Tim, it'll soon pass.'

Then there was the Irishman who bought a ten pound hammer for five pounds because he thought he was getting a half-price bargain.

Fortune teller: You'll meet a tall, dark stranger.
Irish girl: But I don't *know* any strangers, let alone tall dark ones.

Then there was the lazy Irish navvy who had a hernia transplant so he wouldn't have to lift anything heavy.

'Maureen, is Sean hard to please?'
'I don't know, Rosie, I've never tried.'

'You know, Sean, the cleverest invention in the world is the Thermos flask. It keeps hot things hot and cold things cold. But how does it know which is which?'

Definition of an Irish seance. A group of ghosts sitting round a table trying to contact each other.

Why are Irishmen such lousy lovers?
Because they wait for the swelling to go down.

'Hey, Sean, what do you think of Rod Stewart's singing?'
'Oh, it's not as bad as it sounds.'

Disc jockey on Irish radio: I'd tell you the exact time but I've mislaid my script.

Then there was the Irishman who thought Eartha Kitt was a set of gardening tools.

Did you hear about the Irishman who stuck his tongue out at his mother-in-law and missed?

PRISON VISIT

'Good grief, Maureen, every time you come to visit me you're wearing a new expensive coat and new expensive jewellery. At this rate there'll soon be nothing left of the bank raid loot.'

'Oh, Sean, that ran out last month. I'm halfway through the reward money now.'

Did you hear about the Irish pilot who thought an Elastoplast Airstrip was a runway at Heathrow?

CHEMIST SHOP

'Deodorant, please.'
'Ball type, sir?'
'No, it's for my armpits!'

Small ad: House for sale. Within striking distance of local engineering factory.

Then there was the Irishman who thought the Guinness Book of Records was a double-LP of Irish drinking songs.

Dublin scientists have discovered an easy way to split the atom. They'll send it through the Irish Mail marked 'Fragile'.

Three convicts escaped from a Dublin jail. Making their way on foot towards their home town they saw a roadsign which read 'Ballygoorney thirty miles'.

'Thirty miles, that's not far,' exclaimed one. 'It's only ten miles each.'

Irish priest conducting funeral service at graveside: In the name of the Father, in the name of the Son and in-the-hole-he-goes.

'Sean, do you believe we should aim for a total metric system?'

'Oh yes. Every inch of the way!'

Probation officer: Now remember, if you need any help you can phone me between nine and five.
Irish delinquent: I can't stay on the phone all that time. People will be queuing up to use the kiosk.

'Hey, Sean, I heard that your house is dilapidated.'

'That's true. Why?'

'Well, I was just wondering how much those dilapidators charge.'

'Mrs Murphy, why did you have 18 children?'

'Well, to tell the truth, doctor, those kids needed a mother.'

Written on Irish lawnmowers is the warning: 'Keep off the Grass.'

Small ad: Antique card table for sale. No dealers.

Slogan of Irish undertaker: Trust me, I'll be the last person to let you down.

Then there was the Irishman who thought all vending machines were made by a company called Out Of Order.

Letter to school teacher: Dear Teacher, please excuse Tommy from school today as he is unwell. Signed, my Dad.

Then there was the Irish shoplifter who got arrested for stealing free samples.

Irishman: Can you speak?
Parrot: Yes, can you fly?

The stork that brought Murphy was arrested for dope smuggling.

Mrs Murphy was determined to stick to her new diet and to avoid chocolates, cakes, buns and jam tarts. To help matters, she went to her dentist and asked him to remove her sweet tooth.

'Hey, Sean, do you like that group ABBA?'
'Oh yes, especially the one in the middle.'

The KGB tried to brainwash Murphy but couldn't find anywhere to begin.

'Excuse me, Sean, but are you reading that newspaper you're sitting on?'

'Do you have a family, Sean?'
'Indeed I do. Two daughters, both girls.'

An Irish recipe book gives this tip for making iced tea: 'Don't forget to warm the fridge first.'

When Murphy heard that the TV licence detector van was in his neighbourhood, he painted his colour set black and white so he'd get a smaller fine for not having a licence.

'Hey, Sean, here's a good trick to play on someone. You tell 'em you can sell 'em a cigarette lighter and a coat hanger for only ten pence. Then, when you get the money you give them a match and a nail.'

'Oh, that's brilliant, Tim, just brilliant. But if I don't have a match and a nail with me, is it okay to give them my Ronson and a coat hanger instead?'

Irish school children may use pocket calculators in class but only for Latin and English Literature.

I won't say Maureen is stupid but she thought you had to go to a Commissioner For Oaths to be fitted for a Cross Your Heart Bra.

Did you hear about the Irishman who stuck TV licence stamps on his National Insurance card and got 625 fines?

DUBLIN CHEMIST'S SHOP

'Is this insecticide good for ants?'
'Oh no, sir, it's bad for ants. It kills 'em stone dead.'

Then there was the Irishman who was so stupid he thought a law suit was a policeman's uniform.

A Dublin cat breeder has bred a cat which is half Manx and half Persian. The front half is Manx.

Did you hear about the Irishman who went into British Home Stores to buy a house?

Did you hear about the Irishman who thought a corkscrew was a Munster prostitute?

Ireland's best selling novel: *Spuds Lonigan.*

'Tell me, Michael, was it you or your brother who was killed by the hurricane in Florida?'

'I don't know, Sean. Me and Pat were never very close.'

Did you hear about the Irishman who thought Logan's Run was the same sort of ailment as Galloping Gourmet.

Irish disc jockey: Listen carefully to this next record and pay particular attention to the bit five seconds from the end.

'You know, Sean, the price of postage stamps these days is a disgrace.'

'It doesn't affect me because I never put stamps on my letters. I just slip 'em into the pillar box when no one's looking.'

Then there was the Irishman who thought India rubber was a Bombay contraceptive.

Farm sign: For sale. Individually laid eggs.

Then there was the Irish pop composer who wrote a song on blotting paper because it was for the Ink Spots.

IRISH INVENTIONS

WATERPROOF SPONGE
GARLIC FLAVOURED LISTERINE
A DYSLEXIC READING LAMP
A SECURICOR WHEELBARROW
WISDOM DENTURES
DIABETIC EX-LAX
INFLAMMABLE POKER
A BIRO SHARPENER
A MILK GRATER
FILTER TIP CHEWING GUM
A DISTORTING REARVIEW MIRROR
A PAPER PAPERWEIGHT
OPEN TOED WELLIES
AN IRON-ON DEODORANT
CARBONATED TOILET PAPER
INDELIBLE SKY WRITING
FOUR-POSTER SLEEPING BAG
FERTILITY CORN PLASTER
A THOROUGHBRED CLOTHES HORSE
AN I-FART-YOUR-WEIGHT MACHINE
ELECTRIC CHAIR SEAT WARMER
FALSE BITTEN NAILS
A SNOT BANK
TOPLESS BULLETPROOF VEST
A DRIVE-IN BRICK WALL
A POROUS TARPAULIN
THERMAL SUN HAT
AN EAR TROMBONE
ONE-ARM BANDIT FOR THE DISABLED
ROLL-ON TEAR GAS
NATIONAL INSURANCE TAROT CARDS
COALFIRE-POWERED HEARING AID
A HOME FOR UNMARRIED BABIES
A SHIT-POWERED FAN
ROCKING CHAIR SICKNESS PILLS
LIGHTHOUSE MOAT

CAST-IRON PIN CUSHION
EARMUFFS FOR THE INCONTINENT
READY-TO-SERVE TENNIS BALLS
A STRAIGHT-JACKET BOUTIQUE
INFLATABLE SLEDGE HAMMER

Irish TV show: Chips. Series about a potato farmer tracing his roots.

How does an Irish boy scout start a fire?
By rubbing two matches together.

'Doctor, I can't stop telling lies?'
'Do you expect me to believe that?'

Did you hear about the Irish dog who refused to go to obedience school?

'Tim, I think I'm drunk. Help me fall over, will you?'

'Lousy weather, Sean.'
'Yes, but it's better than nothing.'

'Sean, does your dog have fleas?'
'No, but she had pups last week.'

If it's cruel to stick pins in insects, why do they sew zips on flies?

'Father, when you marry Annie and me in church on Saturday, do I stand closer to her than she stands to me or vice versa?'

'Maureen, your tights are wrinkled.'
'I'm not wearing any, Sean.'

Then there was the Irishman who thought manual dexterity was a Mexican film star.

Opinion pollster: Do you believe the age of consent for girls should be lowered to 14?
Mrs Murphy: Certainly. Just as soon as those 14 year-olds become 16.

Irish Treets: They melt in your mouth, not in your shovel.

Murphy was told by his doctor that he needed plenty of roughage. So he got a job as a bouncer.

Did you hear about the Irishman who thought the Benson & Hedges Cup was an ashtray?

'You know, Tommy, when I was your age, every Easter we used to paint funny faces on eggs.'
'Really, Dad? Before or after you fried them?'

'Oh Rosie, this sun tan oil is useless. I've drunk dozens of bottles of the stuff and I'm still as pale as a sheet.'

SURGERY

'Well, Murphy, have you finished that medicine I prescribed for you last time?'
'I haven't even started on it, doctor. The label says to keep the cap screwed tightly on the bottle.'

DUBLIN PUB

First Irish woman: Having another?
Second Irish woman: Glory be, no. It's just the way I've buttoned up this donkey jacket.

Murphy came from a family of winos. In fact, until he was eighteen he thought the opposite of dry was sweet.

Seeing his friend's head tilted back and his eyes crossed, Sean asked Tim what he was doing. Replied Tim, 'I'm looking up my nose to see if I'm wearing my cap.'

'Son, if I've told you once I've told you a million times. Don't exaggerate.'

'Tell me honestly, Sean, could you hit a woman?'
'Sure, send her in!'

'Hey, Sean, you've got a flat tyre.'
'Ah, but it's only flat at the bottom.'

Murphy thought shuttlecock and golf balls, were ailments like tennis elbow and athlete's foot.

Then there was the Irishman who thought aerospace meant the little bubbles in the chocolate bar.

Murphy says he drives his car on the pavement to avoid paying Road Tax.

PHONE CALL TO THE OPERATOR

'Hello, operator? The flex on my phone is far too long. Can you pull it back a bit your end?'

PHONE CALL TO THE DOCTOR

'Doctor, it's Murphy. I've gone blind!'
'You must see a specialist immediately.'

'You know, Maureen, I hate that Terry Wogan.'
'Me too, Molly. I can't stand the sight of listening to him.'

Then there was the Irish mosquito. It died of malaria.

Irishman tossing coin: Best of two!

'Hey, Maureen, why don't you try those new slimming pills?'

'Oh no, Rosie. What with this diet I'm on at the moment, I've got enough on my plate as it is.'

HOTEL PHONE CALL

Irate Guest: Good grief, man, I asked you to give me a seven o'clock alarm call and it's now nine thirty!
Desk clerk: Well, sir, I didn't want the telephone to wake you up!

On her last birthday Maureen received a package in the mail which was a quarter of an inch wide and seventy-five feet long. Inside was a clothes line.

'Sean, it says here in the paper that twenty per cent of all silicon chips manufactured are defective.'

'Ah, Tim, they don't make silicon chips like they used to.'

Sign in Dublin antique shop: Genuine antiques made to order.

What does an Irishman say when he looks in a mirror?
'Snap!'

'Molly, do you prefer men who drink or the other kind?'
'What other kind?'

PHONE CALL TO A POLICE STATION

'Hello. I understand a man's body was found in the Liffey yesterday and so far hasn't been identified?'
'That's correct, yes. Why do you ask?'
'Well, my husband disappeared two days ago and I was wondering if it could be him.'
'Perhaps. Can you tell me anything about your husband which may help to identify him?'
'Yes he has a slight squint in his left eye and talks with a Belfast accent.'

A Dublin cop saw a youth walking down the street wearing a safety pin through his nose. 'Hey,' asked the cop, 'are you a punk rocker?'
'No,' replied the lad, 'I've lost my snot-rag.'

Keep Ireland tidy: When you go on a picnic, put all your litter in a paperbag. Then, on the way home, throw the bag out of the car window.

'Hey, Sean, did you have a good time at Kelly's wake?'
'Yes. Or so they tell me.'

Anyone planning to emigrate to Ireland should take note that the following list of crimes are illegal over there. (Most crimes are illegal in Ireland and those which aren't are against the law.)

Statutory rape, (Unless the statue is over 16)
Recklessly driving a parked car.
Picking your nose while wearing boxing gloves.
Living off immoral IOUs.
Serving alcohol to a newt.
Bribing a police officer with counterfeit money.
Senseless vandalism. (*Sensible* vandalism is permitted).
Escaping from a creditors prison.
Resisting release.
Worrying sheep dogs.
Impersonating a police station.
Allowing your dog to let you foul the pavement.
Making obscene phone boxes.
Exceeding the speed minimum.
Double parking (Unless your car is the one *underneath.*)
Throwing a bucket of water over Siamese twins.
Sprinkling itching powder on fleas.
Divorcing your widow.
Practising medicine without a patient.
Causing a stampede at a silkworm ranch.
Assaulting a corpse. (Unless in self defence.)
Falling awake at a cricket match.
Carrying a concealed flick-shovel.
Waking up a sleeping pill.

'Do you work long hours, Sean?'
'No, just regular 60-minute ones.'

Murphy tried to put in for a No Claims Bonus on his National Insurance.

D'YOU KNOW
WHAT I'D LIKE
TO DO TO YOU?
RIP ALL YOUR
CLOTHES OFF
AND COVER YOU
WITH CUSTARD
AND THEN-
SORRY, GOT TO
GO NOW.
GOODBYE!

What are the qualifications of an Irish brain surgeon?
O level in woodwork.

Ireland's latest craze: Roller skiing.
Ireland's latest food craze: Ice cream burgers.

Then there was the deaf Irishman who had a habit of talking to himself. He looked in the mirror so he could read his lips.

Then there was the Irishman who was invited to a Hunt Ball and asked what the prize was for finding it.

'What, me commit suicide, Sean? I couldn't kill myself to save my life.'

Priest: Murphy, you must cast your bread upon the waters.
Murphy: What? And get soggy bread?

Riley gave his girlfriend so many expensive gifts he finally married her for his money.

Irish cop to hippy: I have reason to believe you smoke pot. Roll up your sleeves!

'Lend me a fiver, Sean, and I'll pay you back that pound I owe you.'

Theatrical agent: So, you want to go into show business doing a memory act? But as you've never tried it before, just how do you expect to remember anything?
Irishman: Simple. I'll tie a piece of string round my little finger.

'You know, Sean, I'll never be able to tell the time if the clocks go metric, too.'

'Doc, people just don't seem to take me seriously.'
'You're kidding.'

'I can't get my new girdle on, Molly.'
'I'm not surprised, Maureen, you've got to wear it a few times before you can get it on.'

DUBLIN PAINT SHOP

'What other colour whitewash do you have?'

'Molly, why are you wearing your wedding ring on the wrong finger?'
'Because, Maureen, I married the wrong man.'

PHONE CALL TO A DOCTOR AT 3 A.M.

Doc: Hello?
Mrs Murphy: Hello.
Doc: Who's speaking?
Mrs M: You are doctor.
Doc: So I am. I thought the voice sounded familiar. Who's that?
Mrs M: Mrs Murphy. You know, *Mr* Murphy's wife.
Doc: Which Mr Murphy?
Mrs M: My husband.
Doc: Oh, him.
Mrs M: I hope I didn't wake you, doctor?
Doc: No, I had to wake up to answer the phone anyway. Well, what's the problem?
Mrs M: It's my son.
Doc: Which one?
Mrs M: The one who's the spitting image of his father ... after he's wiped the spit off. He's taken an overdose of aspirins.
Doc: Is he delirious?
Mrs: M: No, he's Declan.
Doc: But is he in a coma?
Mrs M: No, a camp bed.
Doc: I see, where do you live?
Mrs M: At home.
Doc: Which street?
Mrs M: Galway street.
Doc: What about the number of your house?
Mrs M: It's on the front door.
Doc : I'll make a note of that. Now, if that's all, I'll go back to bed.
Mrs M: But what shall I do about my son who's swallowed an overdose of aspirins?
Doc: Oh, give him a couple of aspirins and I'll be round to see him in the morning.

'You know, Murphy's not as big a fool as he used to be.'
'Why not?'
'He's been on a diet.'

Then there was the deaf and dumb Irishman who broke all his fingers trying to do tongue twisters.

At Irish soccer matches the programmes carry the complete lyrics of *Why Are We Waiting*?

'You know, Tim, when I'm all alone I get very moody.'
'Oh, I'd hate to be with you when you're all alone.'

Then there's the famous Irish birth control pioneer, Dr Michael O'Vary, known as The Father of Sterility.

Did you hear about the Irishman who took his nose to bits to see what made it run?

Then there was the Irish physicist who tried to grow an atomic energy plant in his greenhouse.

Irish cop to suspect: I'm not asking you any questions till my solicitor gets here.

Murphy picked his nose so much he had to get Dyno-Rod to clean out his fingernails.

Irish politician: I believe in dealing with the truth face to face. And I stand behind that statement.

Murphy doesn't know how long he's been out of work because he's lost his birth certificate.

'Is your wife good in bed, Sean?'
'Sure. She phones me from a different one every night.'

QUESTIONS & ANSWERS

Q: What goes red, amber green, green amber, red?
A: A tube of Rowntree's Fruit Gums.

Q: What would you do with a horsechestnut?
A: I'd take it to a throat specialist.

Q: What do you know about computers?
A: He was an ancient Chinese philosopher.

Q: What's the letter 'L' stand for on a car?
A: 'Learner'.
Q: And what does 'GB' mean?
A: Getting better.

Q: What's a yokel?
A: The yellow part of an eggel.

Q: What's a thicket?
A: A bunch of Irish navvies.

Q: Name one of the Seven Wonders of the World.
A: The Eiffel Tower of Pisa.

Q: What's Gaelic for an Irish policewoman?
A: A Seandame.

Explain 'Cyclamate'.
A: It's the passenger on the back of a tandem.

Q: Name two crustaceans.
A: Kings Crustacean and Charing Crustacean.

Q: Explain 'bacteria'.
A: It's the rear entrance to a cafetaria.

Q: Spell turkey.
A: The bird or the country?

Q: What do you know about Moscow?
A: It's where the Kremlin lives.

Q: What's the meaning of the word 'puberty'?
A: It's the age they allow you to go into pubs.

Q: What do you know about atomic waste?
A: It's between your atomic chest and your atomic hips.

Q: What are the four seasons?
A: Salt, mustard, vinegar, pepper.

Q: With which sport do you associate the Ryder cup?
A: Horse racing. Ryder Cup horse to Banbury Cross.

Q: Who were the Western Brothers?
A: Frank and Jesse James.

Q: Name the Dynamic Duo.
A: Raquel Welch.

Q: Give me a sentence using the word 'outwit'.
A: I always get drunk when I'm outwit the lads.

Q: What do you call a very tall Irishman?
A: Paddy Long Legs.

Q: How many seconds in a year?
A: Twelve, January 2nd, February 2nd, March 2nd . . .

THE END

HUMOUR

	ISBN	Author / Title	Price
		Alida Baxter	
	0352398973	**FLAT ON MY BACK**	75p
	0352397187	**OUT ON MY EAR**	75p
	0352397101	**UP TO MY NECK**	75p
	0352301988	**DON'T HANG UP, SOPHIE – IT'S GOD**	60p
	0352303565	**UPSIDE-DOWN UNDER**	85p
		Nicolas Bentley	
	0352301511	**PAY BED**	60p
		Max Bygraves	
	0352301708	**THE MILKMAN'S ON HIS WAY**	75p
		Patrick Campbell	
	0352303662	**MY LIFE AND EASY TIMES**	95p
		Garry Chambers	
	0352304049	**THE (ALMOST) COMPLETE IRISH GAG BOOK**	70p
		John Cleese, Jack Hobbs & Joe McGrath	
Δ	0352301090	**THE STRANGE CASE OF THE END OF CIVILISATION AS WE KNOW IT**	95p
		Rodney Dale	
	0426187105	**THE TUMOUR IN THE WHALE**	75p
		David Dawson	
	0352396245	**VET IN DOWNLAND**	60p
	0352302097	**VET IN THE VALE**	60p
	0352301848	**VET IN THE PADDOCK**	60p
		Les Dawson	
	0352395494	**A CARD FOR THE CLUBS**	60p
	0352397632	**THE SPY WHO CAME**	50p
	0352304316	**THE COSMO SMALLPIECE GUIDE TO MALE LIBERATION**	75p
		Alex Duncan	
	0352398612	**IT'S A VET'S LIFE**	75p
	0352398795	**THE VET HAS NINE LIVES**	75p
	0352395389	**VETS IN CONGRESS**	75p
	0352395699	**VET AMONG THE PIGEONS**	75p
	0352397020	**VETS IN THE BELFRY**	75p
	0352302186	**VET'S CHOICE**	70p
	035230250X	**VET IN THE MANGER**	75p
	035230328X	**VET IN A STATE**	70p
	0352303573	**VET ON VACATION**	75p

† For sale in Britain and Ireland only.
* Not for sale in Canada. • Reissues.
Δ Film & T.V. tie-ins.

HUMOUR

	ISBN	Author / Title	Price
		Dave Dutton	
	0352304235	LANKY SPOKEN HERE	75p
		Ernest Eisler	
	0427004462	THERE WAS A YOUNG LADY (illus)	£2.50p
		Anthony John	
Δ	0352304197	RINGS ON THEIR FINGERS	95p
		Dermot Kennedy	
	0352303433	STUMBLING IN THE AISLES	75p
		Christopher Kenworthy	
Δ	0426186494	CITIZEN SMITH	75p
		Spike Milligan	
	0426157982	A BOOK OF BITS	75p
	0426158199	THE LITTLE POTBOILER	75p
	042615827X	A DUSTBIN OF MILLIGAN	75p
	0426157710	THE BEDSIDE MILLIGAN	75p
	0352397780	THE GREAT McGONAGALL SCRAPBOOK	75p
	0352396407	MILLIGAN'S BOOK OF RECORDS	75p
		Spike Milligan & John Antrobus	
	0426158008	THE BEDSITTING ROOM	75p
	0352303115	THE MORECAMBE & WISE SPECIAL	£1.75
		Stanley Morgan	
	0352395907	A BLOW FOR GABRIEL HORN	70p
	0352396237	INSIDE ALBERT SHIFTY	70p
	0352397454	THE FLY BOYS: SKY-JACKED	70p
	0352395370	RANDY COMFORT RISE AGAIN	70p
	0352395591	RUSS TOBIN: HARD UP	70p
	035230118X	RUSS TOBIN: UP TIGHT	70p
	0352301686	RUSS TOBIN IN HOLLYWOOD	70p
	0352302542	TOBIN AMONG THE STARS	70p
		Frank Muir	
	0352304170	FRANK MUIR GOES INTO . . .	£1.50
		Brendan O'Connor	
	0352303298	FROCK OFF	70p

† For sale in Britain and Ireland only.
* Not for sale in Canada. • Reissues.
Δ Film & T.V. tie-ins.

HUMOUR

THE TWO RONNIES
Edited by Peter Vincent and Ian Davidson

035239899X	THE TWO RONNIES: BUT FIRST THE NEWS	75p
0352301082	MORE OF THE TWO RONNIES: NICE TO BE WITH YOU AGAIN	75p
0352302046	THE TWO RONNIES: IN A PACKED PROGRAMME TONIGHT	75p
0352302496	THE BUMPER BOOK OF THE TWO RONNIES	75p
0352303123	THE TWO RONNIES' SKETCHBOOK (Large Format Illus.)	£1.50
	Spike Mullins	
0352304278	RONNIE IN THE CHAIR	75p
	P. G. Wodehouse	
035230152X	A DAMSEL IN DISTRESS	75p
0352301503	A GENTLEMAN OF LEISURE	75p
0352301694	SOMETHING FISHY	75p
0352301856	UNCLE DYNAMITE	95p
035230197X	COCKTAIL TIME	85p

GAMES & PASTIMES

	Jean Andrew (Editor)	
0426169778	FILL-IN PUZZLES NO. 1	45p*
0426172590	FILL-IN PUZZLES NO. 2	45p*
0426172833	FILL-IN PUZZLES NO. 3	45p*
0426169697	HIDDEN NUMBERS NO. 1	45p
0426172329	HIDDEN WORDS NO. 2	45p*
	'Crosswords Ltd.	
0426169425	CODEWORDS NO. 3	45p*
	Tim Holland	
0352398124	BEGINNING BACKGAMMON	95p
	L. G. Horsefield	
042612829X	CROSSFIGURE PUZZLES NO. 2	60p
0426172248	CROSS-FIGURE PUZZLES NO. 4	50p
	Norman Sullivan	
0426164083	SULLIVAN'S I.Q. TESTS	50p
0352305401	SULLIVAN'S 1ST BOOK OF CROSSWORDS	75p
035230541X	SULLIVAN'S 2ND BOOK OF CROSSWORDS	75p
0352305428	SULLIVAN'S 3RD BOOK OF CROSSWORDS	75p
0352305436	SULLIVAN'S 4TH BOOK OF CROSSWORDS	75p
0352304960	SULLIVAN'S 5TH BOOK OF CROSSWORDS	75p
0426174941	SULLIVAN'S 6TH BOOK OF CROSSWORDS	50p
0426176383	SULLIVAN'S 8TH BOOK OF CROSSWORDS	70p
0427000017	SULLIVAN'S 9TH BOOK OF CROSSWORDS	70p
	(In association with Ideal Home)	
0427000130	LEADERGRAMS	50p

† For sale in Britain and Ireland only.
* Not for sale in Canada. • Reissues.
Δ Film & T.V. tie-ins.